PLEASING GOD JOURNAL

Kay Smith

THE WORD FOR TODAY

P.O. Box 8000, Costa Mesa, CA 92628 • Web Site: www.twft.com • E-mail: info@twft.com

Pleasing God Journal

Published by The Word For Today
P.O. Box 8000, Costa Mesa, CA 92628

Web site: http://www.twft.com
(800) 272-WORD (9673)

© 2008 The Word For Today

ISBN: 978-1-59751-086-8

All rights reserved. No part of this publication may be reproduced, stored in a retrieval system, or transmitted in any form or by any means without the express written consent of The Word For Today Publishers.

Unless otherwise indicated, Scripture quotations in this book are taken from the New King James Version of the Bible. Copyright © 1979, 1980, 1982 by Thomas Nelson, Inc., Publishers. Used by permission. Translational emendations, amplifications, and paraphrases are by the author.

Printed in the United States of America.

Foreword

The *Pleasing God Journal* has been designed to accompany *Pleasing God*, the book written by Kay Smith. Each question can be answered by referring to the text of the *Pleasing God* book and by reading the scriptural references stated within.

This study can be done in a variety of ways. Small weekly groups are ideal for discussion, prayer, and fellowship. The *Pleasing God* book and journal can also be used as an individual study tool and devotion time for personal growth.

To get the most of this study:

Make time.

If possible, set aside a specific time each day to do your study. Consistency is key. Since our busy lives can make it difficult to spend time with the Lord, we need to make sure we give Him a portion of our day to hear from Him.

PRAY.

Ask the Holy Spirit to open your eyes and your heart to behold the wondrous things in His Word. Pray that the truths you learn will be applied to your life and worked out in your attitude and actions.

READ.

Each day, read the assigned portions and meditate on the Scripture to see what the Lord would say to your heart. Be sure to memorize key verses.

STUDY.

You can use other available tools in your study, such as various Bible translations, dictionaries, concordances, and commentaries for further research and insight. However, the best commentary of all is the Holy Spirit.

APPLY.

God has given us a manual for living a life pleasing to God. If we apply the truths we learn, we can have a victorious Christian walk. Application is the key to getting the most from this study.

ATTEND.

If you are doing this study in a group setting, be sure to diligently attend and participate in the discussions and fellowship. If you are new to studying the Bible, don't be concerned if you can't answer every question. You will learn and be encouraged just from hearing other women's answers and experiences.

GROUP LEADER GUIDELINES

As a group leader, your responsibility is not to teach but to:

- Encourage discussion.

- Listen and respond appropriately.

- Facilitate conversation flow and a comfortable atmosphere.

- Clarify any confusing questions or contributions by group members.

- Reduce tension through Spirit-led responses and be ready to mediate any conflict.

- Try to promote participation from every group member, averting one person from monopolizing the conversation.

CHAPTER

1

HOW TO PLEASE GOD

1. As you begin this journal, consider how you can please God. Start by writing Psalm 39:4, personalizing it with your own reflections.

_____
_____
_____
_____

2. God is sending signs and warnings to instruct us how to spend our time on earth. With 2 Peter 3:11 in mind, explain what manner of person you should be in these last days.

_____
_____
_____
_____

3. We can always live in such a way as to please the heart of God. List a few attributes that will characterize this way of life.

   _____
   _____
   _____
   _____

4. To please means to delight, satisfy, or gratify. What is the difference between doing things for God out of obedience rather than from a desire to please Him?

   _____
   _____
   _____
   _____

5. According to Revelation 4:11, we were created for God's pleasure. If we choose to please ourselves in place of God, what will result?

   _____
   _____
   _____
   _____

6. Why does Hebrews 11:5 testify that Enoch pleased God? Also refer to Genesis 5:24 to assist you in your answer.

   _____
   _____
   _____
   _____

7. Women often look to others for approval or appreciation. Why will a fullness of joy result from pleasing God in comparison to pleasing yourself or others?

8. Society influences us to invite popular friends over for dinner so we will be invited back! Write Jesus' invitation recommendations. See Luke 14:12-14.

9. Matthew 22:37 says, "You shall love the LORD your God with all your heart, soul and mind." Give some practical examples of how you show your love for God.

10. What is your response to Satan's lie that "a life lived to please God is boring and unfulfilling"? State Scripture to support your answer.

11. It's inevitable that when we choose to please God, we're going to fail in some areas. What's the remedy found in 1 John 1:9?

_____
_____
_____
_____
_____

12. When we're consumed with God's love, we won't seem to notice unpleasantness that might bog us down. Cite an example from your own life that demonstrates this type of response.

_____
_____
_____
_____
_____

Finally then, brethren, we urge and exhort in the Lord Jesus that you should abound more and more, just as you received from us how you ought to walk and to please God.
- 1 Thessalonians 4:1

Personal Notes

Personal Notes

CHAPTER

2

DOES THIS PLEASE GOD?

1. Jesus said, "I always do those things that please Him" (John 8:29). What does this statement mean to you?

   _____
   _____
   _____
   _____

2. Share a few personal examples of how you are living to please God this week.

   _____
   _____
   _____
   _____

3. Knowing the end times are at hand, why would you ask yourself, "Does this please God?" before reading a book or watching a TV program or movie?

_____
_____
_____
_____

4. A recent poll claimed ninety-six percent of Americans believe in God; however, James 2:19 says "even the demons believe—and tremble!" To please God, what more must we do than simply believe?

_____
_____
_____
_____

5. The heroes of faith listed in Hebrews 11 believed in a personal God Who watched and cared for them. How does their faith inspire you to please God?

_____
_____
_____
_____

6. Psalm 139:17-18 expresses that God's thoughts toward you are more than the sands of the sea. Please God by writing your thoughts about Him.

_____
_____
_____
_____

7. Why does it please God when you have a continual awareness of His presence?

8. When unbelievers call on the Lord in their desperate times, does God hear? Does it please Him? Share a Scripture that supports your answer.

9. If someone were to ask you, "How can I know God?" what would be your answer?

10. Without faith, it's impossible to please God; yet, God rewards those who diligently seek Him. Contribute at least four ways you can live to please God.

Personal Notes

Personal Notes

Personal Notes

CHAPTER

3

DEAD TO SIN

1. If you want a life that is pleasing to God, consider Him first. State one choice you have made differently this week considering God's desire from you.

_____
_____
_____
_____

2. If you desire to please God, acknowledge what doesn't please Him. Paraphrase Hebrews 11:6 recognizing what displeases God.

_____
_____
_____
_____

3. Romans 8:8 declares, "They that are in the flesh cannot please God." Expound upon what it means to be in the flesh.

_____
_____
_____
_____

4. Romans 6:6 declares that when temptation arises, you don't have to succumb to it. Sin and selfishness have no power over you. Why is this truth liberating?

_____
_____
_____
_____

5. First Corinthians 6:19-20 holds the key to understanding why you are free from sin. Write it here.

_____
_____
_____
_____

6. Romans 6:11 exhorts to "reckon yourself to be dead indeed to sin, but alive to God in Christ Jesus." You have the choice to yield to your flesh—and sin—or to be obedient. If you are filled with the Holy Spirit, how will this help you to walk in obedience?

_____
_____
_____
_____

7. There are things you can do—and are responsible to do—if you are to overcome sinful desires. Read the following Scriptures and state your responsibility.

   a. Romans 13:14. If you are not able to walk the victorious life in Christ, who is to blame?

   b. Galatians 5:16. Explain walking after the Spirit.

   c. Colossians 3:5. How do you put to death your members?

   d. First Peter 2:11. What does the term "abstain" mean to you?

   e. First Corinthians 6:18a. How does this relate to what you see on TV and in the movies?

f. Second Timothy 2:19b. What is the definite admonishment from God to you?

_____
_____
_____

g. Second Timothy 2:22. How are you to handle lust?

_____
_____
_____

8. Can people look at you and tell you are a Christian? First Corinthians 6:20 states, "Glorify God in your body and in your spirit, which are God's." How do you glorify God in your body and in your spirit?

_____
_____
_____
_____
_____
_____
_____

Therefore do not let sin reign in your mortal body, that you should obey it in its lusts. And do not present your members as instruments of unrighteousness to sin, but present yourselves to God as being alive from the dead, and your members as instruments of righteousness to God. For sin shall not have dominion over you, for you are not under law but under grace.

- Romans 6:12-14

Personal Notes

Personal Notes

CHAPTER

4

A Pattern for Change

1. God's Word is full of patterns to help you please Him. If you meet God's condition, His promise will change your life. What is the condition and promise found in the following Scriptures to help you change?

   a. Proverbs 3:7-8

   ———————————————————————
   ———————————————————————

   b. Matthew 6:33

   ———————————————————————
   ———————————————————————

   c. Luke 6:38

   ———————————————————————
   ———————————————————————

2. Psalm 37:1-7 gives the pattern to stop fretting. List the conditions and promises to help you change.

   _____
   _____
   _____
   _____

3. James 4:1-10 is another life-changing pattern. Complete the following verses to give you understanding.

   a. "You do not have because _____."

   b. "Whoever chooses to be a friend of the world _____."

   c. "God sets Himself against the proud and haughty, but _____."

   d. "Come close to God and _____."

   e. "Humble yourselves in the presence of the Lord, and _____."

4. Seven biblical patterns have been prearranged to change your life. Pattern 1 is to recognize your sin and confess it. Referring to James 4:1-10, write the verses that help you recognize sin.

   _____
   _____
   _____
   _____

5. Pattern 2 is in James 4:7a. Write this verse and share practical ways to implement this change into your life.

_____
_____
_____
_____

6. Pattern 3 is "Resist the Devil and he will flee from you." Write how you can apply this pattern in your life. Refer to 1 Peter 5:8-9 to help with your answer.

_____
_____
_____
_____

7. Pattern 4 is "Draw near to God and He will draw near to you" (James 4:8a). What are some ways you can draw near to God every day?

_____
_____
_____
_____

8. Read and write Pattern 5 found in James 4:8b. What are your thoughts in relation to this important instruction?

_____
_____
_____
_____

9. James 4:9 says to "lament and mourn and weep" over your sin. Why is this a good pattern to follow in order to please God?

_____
_____
_____
_____
_____

10. The final pattern is found in James 4:10. Write it here and explain the difference between having low self-esteem and realizing your utter worthlessness apart from God.

_____
_____
_____
_____
_____
_____
_____
_____

Therefore submit to God. Resist the devil and he will flee from you. Draw near to God and He will draw near to you. Cleanse your hands, you sinners; and purify your hearts, you double-minded. Lament and mourn and weep! Let your laughter be turned to mourning and your joy to gloom. Humble yourselves in the sight of the Lord, and He will lift you up.

- James 4:7-10

Personal Notes

Personal Notes

CHAPTER

5

WALK WITH GOD

1. Before you begin your study, take a 15-minute stroll and talk with God. Paraphrase your conversation and share what revelation the Holy Spirit gave to you.

   _____
   _____
   _____
   _____

2. In your quest to please God, you realize that walking with Him is pleasing. Read Hebrews chapter 11 and record some godly examples of those who faithfully walked with God.

   _____
   _____
   _____

3. When you walk with someone, you will trust and know them better. Clarify why reading the Bible daily will help your walk with God. Give Scripture to support your answer.

4. As you read about Enoch's example in Genesis 5:22a, 24, it reveals his secret to pleasing God. Define what this means to you.

5. Genesis 6:9 reveals someone else who walked with God and describes his character. What does it say?

6. In Ephesians 6:15, what does God tell you to wear as you walk with Him, and why is this important?

7. This desire to walk with God goes beyond obedience—it's a desire to please Him. Why is a true love for God necessary to walk with Him?

_____
_____
_____
_____

8. Why will your perspective change when you walk with God?

_____
_____
_____
_____

9. Write the walking promise found in Deuteronomy 5:33.

_____
_____
_____
_____

10. Commit to taking more walks with God. How can you arrange your priorities to spend more time walking with Him? Write your commitment.

_____
_____
_____
_____
_____

Personal Notes

Personal Notes

Personal Notes

CHAPTER
6
A LIVING SACRIFICE

1. A religious Jew celebrates *Yom Kippur*, the Day of Atonement. It was a foreshadowing of Jesus becoming the sacrifice to cover our sins. Today, if you decided to sacrifice something for Jesus, what would it be?

   _____
   _____
   _____
   _____

2. According to Jesus' teaching on prayer in Matthew 5:23-24, what do you need to "sacrifice" before you come into the presence of God?

   _____
   _____
   _____
   _____

3. Reflect upon Jesus' sacrifice for you. How should you respond according to Romans 12:1?

_____
_____
_____
_____

4. The word "body" means the whole person—body, soul, and spirit. What does it mean to present your body a living sacrifice to Jesus Christ?

_____
_____
_____
_____

5. Write 1 Thessalonians 4:1. What is the Holy Spirit impressing upon your heart to abound more and more in your life?

_____
_____
_____
_____

6. Read 1 Corinthians 3:16-17. In what practical ways can you adhere to the exhortation to keep your body a living sacrifice?

_____
_____
_____
_____

7. Pleasing God involves presenting your mind to God. Ephesians 4:23 declares, "Be renewed in the spirit of your mind." How do you present your mind to God?

_____
_____
_____
_____

8. Job 5:2 is a good description of uncontrolled emotions. What do out-of-control emotions do to a person?

_____
_____
_____
_____

9. Matthew 26:13 inscribes a memorial relevant today. What is the significance of this woman's sacrifice for Jesus?

_____
_____
_____
_____

10. God will not force you, but your sacrifice represents your deepest desire to please Him. Pray for the Holy Spirit to show you what would be a pleasing sacrifice unto the Lord. Write your commitment here.

_____
_____
_____
_____

Personal Notes

Personal Notes

Personal Notes

CHAPTER

7

LOVE NOT THE WORLD

1. By living to please God, you can become the strongest influence possible in this world. Write out Romans 12:2 and underline the seven words given to help you attain this goal.

   _____
   _____
   _____
   _____

2. The apostles Paul and John give us strong exhortations about this world. What worldly temptations does Satan use to entice you? See 1 John 2:16.

   _____
   _____
   _____
   _____

3. We may conform to this world, mistakenly thinking that by doing so our needs will be met. What is Jesus' wonderful promise found in Matthew 6:33?

4. Too many people think they can love God and also love the things this world offers. Write the truth stated in James 4:4, and note your concerns.

5. When your spiritual eyes are open to the fleeting, phony, competitive, selfish values of this world, you will have no love for it. Personalize Paul's declaration in Galatians 6:14b.

6. What does 1 John 2:17 say will happen to this world's system, and what happens when you do the will of God?

7. In the columns write words that describe the world's ideal woman, and then choose words that illustrate God's ideal of a Christian woman. Refer to 1 Peter 3:3-4 to aid in your answer.

WORLD'S IDEAL	GOD'S IDEAL

8. We live in a world whose motto is: "Me first." Why is this attitude displeasing to God?

9. Ask yourself this question to see if you are being conformed to this world: "What do I really enjoy doing when I have some free time?" Write your answer and share your thoughts.

10. Evaluate your goals. The goal of the apostle Paul is established in Philippians 3:10. You can find King David's aim in Psalm 17:15. What is your goal or aim today?

___

Do not love the world or the things in the world. If anyone loves the world, the love of the Father is not in him. For all that is in the world—the lust of the flesh, the lust of the eyes, and the pride of life—is not of the Father but is of the world. And the world is passing away, and the lust of it; but he who does the will of God abides forever.

- 1 John 2:15-17

Personal Notes

Personal Notes

CHAPTER

8

Renew Your Mind

1. Read Romans 12:2 and define the words "transform" and "renew." What is the spiritual significance?

   _____
   _____
   _____
   _____

2. As illustrated in 2 Kings 5:1-14, God doesn't desire a quick fix to renew your mind, but asks you to seek His Holy Spirit. Write a prayer asking for His help.

   _____
   _____
   _____
   _____

3. After identifying the world's ideal woman in contrast to God's best for you, read Philippians 2:5-8. Share how your mind can be transformed and renewed by observing Jesus as your model.

_____
_____
_____
_____
_____

4. As the Holy Spirit works in your life, you have a part as well—to cooperate. Colossians 3:2 is a great place to start. Write it here as you memorize and imprint it upon your heart.

_____
_____
_____
_____
_____

5. What you think upon is what you become. Proverbs 23:7 exposes your character in your conversations with other people. How can you renew your thoughts to improve your speech?

_____
_____
_____
_____
_____

6. God chose your mind as the starting point for spiritual regeneration. Read Romans chapter 1 and share the verse(s) the Holy Spirit has imparted especially to you.

_____
_____
_____
_____
_____

7. When you present your entire self to the Lord, His Holy Spirit can renew your desires and attitudes to be pleasing to Him. List some of these praiseworthy thoughts listed in Philippians 4:8.

_____
_____
_____
_____
_____

8. Reflect upon Psalm 1:1-3 and write the promise for the one who thinks on the right things.

_____
_____
_____
_____
_____
_____

9. If you find it's a battle to cease from thinking wrong thoughts or fantasies, carry 2 Corinthians 10:4-5 in your spiritual arsenal. Write it here and commit it to memory.

_____
_____
_____
_____
_____

10. In Psalm 139:23-24 David prayed, "Search me, God, and know my heart … know my thoughts." Take a moment and write a prayer asking God to search you and to dispose of any displeasing thoughts and to renew your mind.

_____
_____
_____
_____
_____
_____
_____
_____

And do not be conformed to this world, but be transformed by the renewing of your mind, that you may prove what is that good and acceptable and perfect will of God.

- Romans 12:2

Personal Notes

Personal Notes

CHAPTER

9

THE HEART OF WORSHIP

1. Worship is a loving response to the living God. Your concept of God will reveal your worship. What is your belief and your concept of God?

   _____
   _____
   _____
   _____

2. How do you know if your worship is what God desires? Read John 4:23-24 and write in your own words how God wants you to worship.

   _____
   _____
   _____
   _____

3. Learning from Elisabeth and Mary's example of worship in Luke 1:39-55, what words and phrases stand out to include in your worship of the Lord?

_____
_____
_____
_____

4. As you worship God and focus on His power and ability, how will this help you in times of tribulation, trial, and trouble?

_____
_____
_____
_____

5. The first step in learning how to worship God in a way that would please Him is simply to ask. Write a prayer asking the Lord to teach you how to worship Him.

_____
_____
_____
_____

6. Use a Bible concordance and look up the words, "worship," "praise," and "thanksgiving." Begin a list of verses here, and write your favorite Scriptures in the *Personal Notes* section at the end of this chapter.

_____
_____
_____
_____

7. Observing Psalm 95 as a teaching tool, discover the different methods of worship. What are some ways to worship found in Psalm 95:1-6?

8. Psalm 95 not only gives different ways to worship, but it also lists many truths about God. Make a list of what you learn about Him in this psalm.

9. Why did the woman in Luke 7:36-50 worship Jesus? How is she an example to you?

10. True, reverent worship can be manifested in the midst of heavy trials. What was Job's response during his difficult trials in Job 1:21? What do you learn from Job's example?

Personal Notes

Personal Notes

Personal Notes

CHAPTER
10
WALK IN LOVE

1. It is pleasing to God when you walk in love. When you are buffeted for something in which you are not guilty, 1 Peter 2:20 is a good reminder about how to respond. Write it in your own words.

_____
_____
_____
_____

2. First Corinthians 13:4-7 gives a beautiful definition of love. What is *agape* love and why is it necessary to practice this type of love?

_____
_____
_____
_____

3. According to Ephesians 4:31-32, what do you need to "put away" in order to walk in His love? What specific instruction is given about forgiveness?

___

4. As you meditate on Jeremiah 17:9, why isn't it very wise to trust your feelings or the motives of your heart? How could this be potentially harmful?

___

5. The gifts of the Spirit listed in 1 Corinthians 12:8-10 are impressive, yet are useless if they are not motivated by love. How does 1 Corinthians 13:1-3 challenge you to walk in love?

___

6. Like the wind, God's *agape* love is invisible—you can only feel the results of it. Read John 13:34-35 and explain how people will know you are Jesus' disciple.

___

7. When you read John 17:9, 20 you perceive that Jesus is praying for the disciples who walk with Him—including you! Who walks with you? List their names and a short prayer request for them.

_____
_____
_____
_____
_____

8. We read in John 6:3 that despite so many people around Jesus, He spent time alone with His disciples. Love invests time in others. List some ways you can exemplify the love of Jesus by giving of your time this week.

_____
_____
_____
_____
_____

9. Matthew 10:29-31 confirms how much your heavenly Father is aware of you and cares for you—down to the very hairs of your head. How might you be able to confirm your love to others too?

_____
_____
_____
_____
_____

10. Jesus demonstrated His *agape* love in very tangible ways (John 21:9-12), and by putting others first (Philippians 2:6-8). Beholding His example, how can you demonstrate your love practically to those around you?

_____
_____
_____
_____

11. In Isaiah 6:1-5, the prophet is reminded of the magnificence and holiness of God, which produced a humility within him. How does this help you to walk in love today?

_____
_____
_____
_____

12. John 15:13 reads, "Greater love has no one than this, than to lay down one's life for his friends." This Scripture is the ultimate example of walking in love. Name the qualities you would like to see from your own life as proof that you walk in love.

_____
_____
_____
_____

And now abide faith, hope, love, these three; but the greatest of these is love.
- 1 Corinthians 13:13

Personal Notes

Personal Notes

CHAPTER

11

Love Your Enemies

1. This chapter goes a step further than just walking in love—we're going to study how to love our enemies. God never asks us to do something that He is not willing to do Himself. Use John 3:16 to describe the people God loves.

   _____
   _____
   _____
   _____

2. God is kind and patient to draw us to Him, and when we do the same it pleases Him. In Matthew 5:44, how does God want us to behave toward our enemies?

   _____
   _____
   _____
   _____

3. Jesus said we are to love our enemies. Describe what this kind of *agape* love looks like according to 1 Corinthians 13:4-7.

_____
_____
_____
_____

4. Your enemies may cause problems in your life, but God can use these circumstances for you to represent Him. How did Joseph represent God in Genesis 50:20?

_____
_____
_____
_____

5. Writing down your decision to love your enemies is a good way to affirm it. Take a moment and write a prayer for a person you are struggling to love.

_____
_____
_____
_____

6. God provides the help to love our enemies. What assurance does He give in John 14:16-18 and Romans 5:5?

_____
_____
_____
_____

7. Many times we want to defend and justify ourselves with our enemies. How do the following Scriptures help you to trust God to defend you?

   a. Psalm 56:3

   b. Psalm 56:4

   c. Psalm 27:5

   d. Psalm 31:20

8. One practical step to loving your enemy is refusal to do anything vengeful. Record what you learn in 1 Peter 3:12 to help you keep your attitude and actions pleasing to the Lord.

9. Jesus is our model for loving our enemies—He blessed those who cursed Him. What does Romans 12:17-20 add to this principle?

10. Loving your enemy is beneficial. Read Matthew 5:44-45 and note the result of loving your enemy according to verse 45. How has this changed your perspective toward those who are unkind to you?

I say to you, love your enemies, bless those who curse you, do good to those who hate you, and pray for those who spitefully use you and persecute you.

- Matthew 5:44

Personal Notes

Personal Notes

CHAPTER
12
Everything unto Jesus

1. Take a moment and write down everything you need to do today. Now look at your list; what matters most to you?

　
　
　
　

2. Read John 12:1-7. Write down your thoughts as to why Mary sacrificed everything unto Jesus.

3. Mark 14:3-9 is another account of Mary's sacrifice to Jesus. Why do you think Jesus said her act of love would be told as a memorial to her?

_____

_____

_____

_____

_____

4. As we reflect on Mary's gift to Jesus in Mark 14:3, we notice that she broke the alabaster flask of perfumed oil to use for Jesus. Why is brokenness in your life a precious fragrance to Him?

_____

_____

_____

_____

_____

5. Mary's beautiful act produced sharp criticism from others in the room. Can you think of a specific time when you were criticized for giving something to Jesus? What happened?

_____

_____

_____

_____

_____

6. In Mark 14:6-8, how did Jesus commend Mary's courageous act? How do you think Jesus commends you today when you give everything unto Him?

_____

7. In 1 Corinthians 11:15, the apostle Paul wrote that a woman's hair is her glory, pride, and joy. When Mary wiped the feet of Jesus with her hair, what was the significance of her action?

_____

8. One of your costliest possessions is your time. Express what it means for you to spend time alone with Jesus as you live to please Him.

_____

9. Review the following passages recognizing that each account was written with you in mind. Write your response realizing that Jesus gave everything to you:

   a. Matthew 26-28

   _____
   _____

   b. Mark 14-16

   _____
   _____

   c. Luke 22-24

   _____
   _____

   d. John 12-20

   _____
   _____

10. Let the magnitude of what Jesus did for you inspire a deep and intimate love for Him. What can you sacrifice to Jesus today that signifies giving everything you have to Him?

   _____
   _____
   _____
   _____

But as you abound in everything—in faith, in speech, in knowledge, in all diligence, and in your love for us—see that you abound in this grace also.
- 2 Corinthians 8:7

Personal Notes

Personal Notes

CHAPTER 13

PRAISE AND FEAR THE LORD

1. How well do you know God? In this chapter we are going to find out how to know God through His Word. What is the first thing you learn in Psalm 34:1 that will please God?

_____
_____
_____
_____

2. Read Psalm 34:2. When you praise the Lord and give thanks for what He has done, what happens to the humble? What will help you when you are discouraged and afflicted?

_____
_____
_____
_____

3. Many times we pray from a point of fear rather than from a place of trust. Why is fear the opposite of faith?

___

4. As you praise and fear the Lord, what effect does it have on others? See Psalm 34:5.

___

5. Compare Psalm 34:4 with Psalm 34:6. Relate how this speaks to you about the deliverance of the Lord.

___

6. An awareness of God's presence can be the difference between being fearful and being at peace. Write out Psalm 34:7 and commit it to memory. How will this promise enable you to praise the Lord in times of need?

___

7. Psalm 34:9 tells us, "Oh, fear the Lord, you His saints! There is no want to those who fear Him." What is meant by the word "fear"? What does this look like in your life?

___

8. Today our society has a casual attitude towards sin, resulting from a lack of respect towards God. Write Proverbs 8:13 and 16:6 and share what you learn from these verses.

___

9. The fear of the Lord begins with your mouth. What specific instructions are given in Psalm 34:13? What is your response to the nudge of the Holy Spirit when you start to say something questionable?

___

10. Psalm 34:14 says, "Depart from evil and do good." Ask God to put His searchlight on your life and write what He is showing you to depart from—then repent and do good.

_____
_____
_____
_____

11. When conflict or tension arises over a situation, what response would be praiseworthy to God? See Psalm 34:14b for your answer and write how you can make this applicable to your life.

_____
_____
_____
_____

12. Read the rest of Psalm 34. As you've read through these verses, it's likely the Holy Spirit has been speaking to you about something specific. Be honest before Him and confess whatever He's shown you. Write your prayer of thanksgiving to Him here.

_____
_____
_____
_____

Oh, taste and see that the LORD is good; blessed is the man who trusts in Him! Oh, fear the LORD, you His saints! There is no want to those who fear Him.

~ Psalm 34:8-9

Personal Notes

Personal Notes

CHAPTER

14

Parable of the Sower

1. Why do some Christians wither away while others bloom and grow? In Mark 4:1-20, Jesus used the parable of the sower to teach about four different types of soil (representing four different heart conditions). List the four types of soil and what they represent.

_____
_____
_____
_____

2. According to Luke 8:11, what does the seed represent to us spiritually?

_____
_____
_____
_____

3. What happens after the Word of God is sown in the wayside heart? Refer to Luke 8:5, Mark 4:15, and Matthew 13:19.

___

4. The second type of soil is stony ground (Mark 4:5-6). What causes the Word of God to wither away in a stony heart?

___

5. The third type of soil is thorny ground that used to be good soil, but became covered with thorns. Referring to Mark 4:19, what do those thorns represent? Why do thorns harm a Christian?

___

6. What prevents the Word from taking root in a person's heart? How can you avoid unfruitfulness in your Christian life? Read Mark 4:18-19.

___

7. Anxious thoughts and financial worries are some of the thorns that choke out fruitfulness. Rather than allowing these "thorns" to come into your life, what is the remedy according to Matthew 6:33?

_____
_____
_____
_____
_____

8. God has given "all things that pertain to life and godliness" (2 Peter 1:3); yet sometimes we choose to sit down among the thorns. Ask the Lord for wisdom in this area to see what thorns are around you. Write them here.

_____
_____
_____
_____
_____

9. Why did Jesus speak about the deceitfulness of riches? Write out Psalm 62:10 and explain what could happen to your heart. What would be good advice if you become wealthy?

_____
_____
_____
_____
_____

10. The best kind of soil is described in Mark 4:8. What is the key to having a heart that yields an abundant, fruitful crop?

___

11. John 15:8 tells us, "By this My Father is glorified, that you bear much fruit." Name some ways you can bear fruit to please Jesus.

___

12. Write a prayer asking the Lord to plant His Word deeply in your heart and to show you how to bear much fruit for Him.

___

But other seed fell on good ground and yielded a crop that sprang up, increased and produced: some thirtyfold, some sixty, and some a hundred.

~ Mark 4:8

Personal Notes

Personal Notes

CHAPTER
15
Remember

1. Psalm 143:5 says, "I remember the days of old; I meditate on all Your works." Spend a few moments remembering God's goodness and care for you as you have learned to please Him. Write it here.

_____
_____
_____
_____

2. While God desires for you to remember, He also wants you to forget feelings of condemnation and guilt. Read Philippians 3:7-14 and note what it means to you "to forget those things which are behind."

_____
_____
_____

3. The apostle Paul needed to forget not only his past sins, but also his past achievements. Philippians 3:7-8 says by counting all things loss, we gain something far greater. What do we gain?

_____

_____

_____

_____

4. Referring to Psalm 103:3-5, list some of God's marvelous works, which are good for you to remember.

_____

_____

_____

_____

5. After crossing the Jordan River, the Israelites built a memorial of stones in order to recall God's miracles to their children (Joshua 4:6). How are you sharing God's wonderful works with your children or with the next generation?

_____

_____

_____

_____

6. Read Exodus 23:14 and write what God established for the children of Israel to help them remember what He had done for them.

_____

_____

_____

_____

7. God used the Feast of Booths to remind the Israelites of three specific things. What did God want them to remember? See Leviticus 23:43.

_____
_____
_____
_____
_____

8. The Feast of Booths represented God's providential care for the Jews during the forty years in the wilderness. In Deuteronomy 34:7, what was God's "providential care"?

_____
_____
_____
_____
_____

9. God asked the children of Israel to make a frail booth to remind them—and us—that we are only in temporary dwellings. How does 1 Corinthians 15:52-53 support this reminder?

_____
_____
_____
_____
_____
_____

10. Rather than worrying about how well your tent (body) is holding up or what it looks like, what does 1 Peter 3:3-4 exhort you to do?

___

11. Second Corinthians 4:18 helps you to be mindful that "the things which are seen are temporary, but the things which are not seen are eternal." How does this help you to remember the things you've learned that please God?

___

12. In conclusion, write a prayer of praise and thanksgiving for God's great love for you. Ask the Holy Spirit to keep you sensitive to His work in your life in order that you may please Him every day.

___

Now may the God of peace ... make you complete in every good work to do His will, working in you what is well pleasing in His sight, through Jesus Christ, to whom be glory forever and ever. Amen.

Hebrews 13:20-21

Personal Notes

Personal Notes

Personal Notes

Personal Notes

Personal Notes

Personal Notes